Let's Take a Trip
The Everglades

by Cheryl Koenig Morgan

photography by the author

Troll Associates

Library of Congress Cataloging-in-Publication Data

Morgan, Cheryl Koenig.
   The Everglades / by Cheryl Koenig Morgan; photography
by Cheryl Koenig Morgan.
       p.   cm.—(Let's take a trip)
   Summary: Describes the plant and animal life found in the
Everglades National Park.
   ISBN 0-8167-1733-8 (lib. bdg.)   ISBN 0-8167-1734-6 (pbk.)
   1. Everglades National Park (Fla.)—Juvenile literature.
2. Natural history—Florida—Everglades National Park—Juvenile
literature.   3. Everglades National Park (Fla.).—Pictorial works—
Juvenile literature.   4. Natural history—Florida—Everglades
National Park—Pictorial works—Juvenile literature.
[1. Everglades National Park (Fla.)   2. Natural history—Florida—
Everglades National Park.   3. National parks and reserves.]
I. Title. II. Series.
F317.E9M67 1990
917.59 '39—dc20   89-5175

10 9 8 7 6 5 4 3 2 1

The author and publisher wish to thank Shirley Beccue, Kim King, David Eastham, and the rest of the
staff at Everglades National Park for their generous assistance and to acknowledge the National
Park Service/Mike Giannechini for the photograph of a crocodile on page 28.

One of the wettest places in the United States is a vast region in Florida called the Everglades. At the southern tip of this huge area lies Everglades National Park. The park's Visitor Center is a good place to begin a trip through the Everglades. The park's rangers are happy to provide us with information and get us off on the right foot!

Our first stop is the Anhinga Trail. The trail
follows a man-made canal to a wooden boardwalk
built over a fresh-water *slough*. A slough is a deep
channel that flows slowly through the saw grass
prairie, or flat lands. A display shows some of the
birds, fish, and other animals to look for along the
trail.

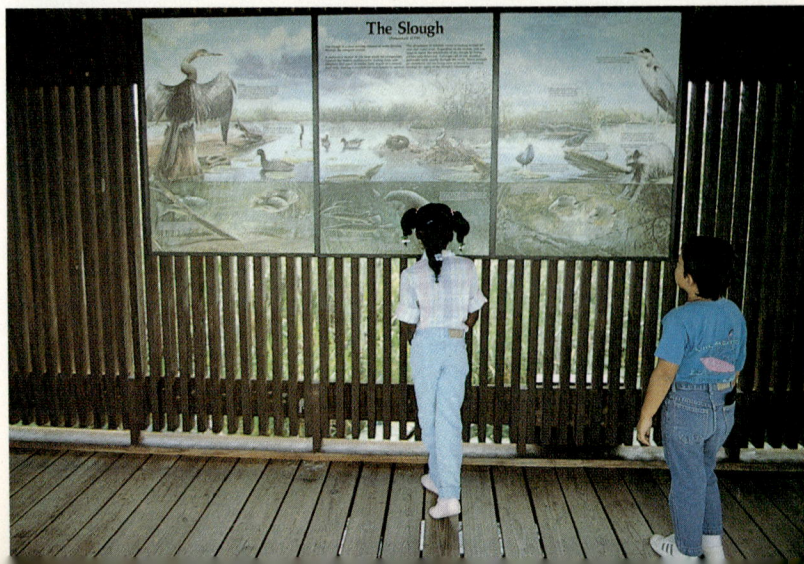

Birds are the most common animals on the Anhinga Trail. Ranger Shirley shows how to use a guidebook and binoculars to identify the bird for which the trail is named. The anhinga's wings are not waterproof, so it has trouble flying when wet. To dry itself, it perches on a branch with its wings outstretched.

Fishing
Reserved
For The Birds

DO NOT
FEED THE
WILDLIFE

Birds that live in Everglades National Park are skilled at catching fish. One of the more common birds here is the great blue heron. Its eyes are pointed downward because that's where the fish are! People are not permitted to feed the birds and other wildlife in any of the waters of Everglades National Park.

The white ibis is easy to recognize because of its curved orange bill. Indians once hunted this bird for food, but laws now protect it and other wild birds. The brightly colored purple gallinule is very rare. Among its favorite spots are the ponds along the Anhinga Trail, where it is sometimes seen hunting for fish, worms, and seeds of water plants.

Alligators may be the most famous residents of Everglades National Park. From the Anhinga Trail, they can be seen at the water's edge or using their powerful tails to propel themselves through the water. After young alligators hatch from eggs, they live with their mothers for a year before going off on their own.

As in all of nature, every animal in the Everglades depends on some other living thing for food. Turtles eat the pond apples that fall from trees into the water. Birds eat fish. Alligators eat birds and turtles, while young alligators often eat tiny apple snails. In the rainy summer season, marsh rabbits nibble on grass along the trail.

All the plants and animals in the Everglades are part of an *ecosystem*—a web of life in which everything is delicately balanced. Dragonflies depend on mosquitos for food, so if there were no mosquitos, these "mosquito dragons" might also disappear. The golden orb spider spins huge webs—up to three feet across—to catch the insects on which it feeds. The webs are so strong that they have been made into bags and fish nets.

The largest grasshopper in the United States—the
two-inch-long lubber grasshopper—lives in the
Everglades. Like other grasshoppers, the lubber
eats plants. The green anole is a lizard that
prefers to eat insects. Anoles can change color,
turning from bright green to brown or gray.

Another trail in Everglades National Park is the Gumbo-Limbo Trail, which leads through a subtropical forest on one of the park's *hammocks*. A hammock is a tree island covered with damp, dense vegetation. Ranger Kim shows Sam the gumbo-limbo tree, with its large roots and peeling red bark. The light wood of this tree was once used to make carousel horses. Many animals, such as tree frogs, live in the trees.

The tree snails that glide along tree branches in the forest have shells that may be all white or colorfully striped. Shield ferns and delicate mushrooms may be seen growing on the forest floor. The plants and animals found in different parts of the Everglades give each trail its own character and personality.

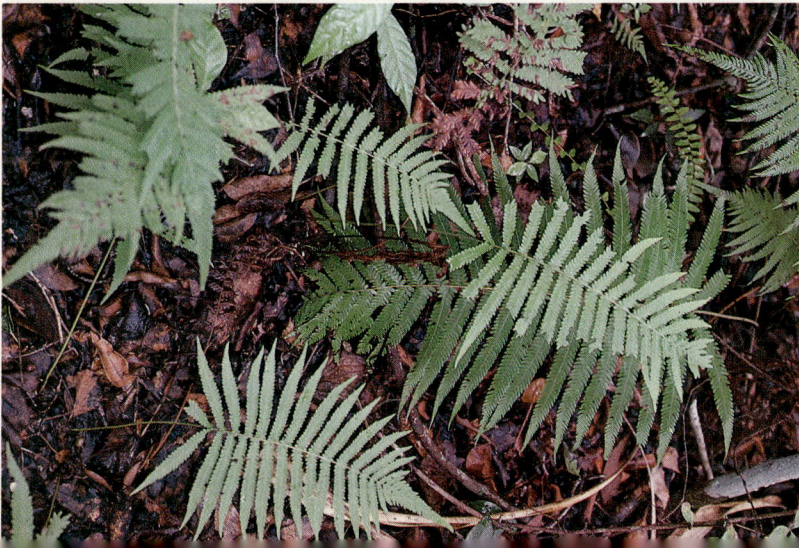

The next habitat we come upon is very different from the subtropical forest of the Gumbo-Limbo Trail. It is an island called *Long Pine Key*. The word *key* comes from the Spanish word for island—*cayo*. Here the higher elevation supports a forest of southern slash pine that is full of birds, deer, and snakes. Twenty-four different kinds of snakes live in the Everglades, but only four are poisonous. This rare eastern indigo snake is nonpoisonous.

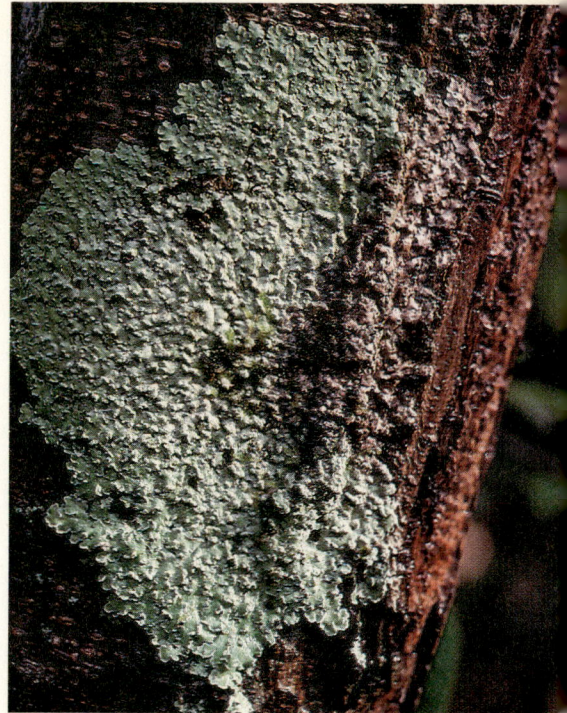

Many plants and insects also live in the pine forest. The bright red coral bean flower attracts a sulphur butterfly. *Lichen*, a tiny plant that was once widely used to make antibiotic medicines, grows on pine trees. The pretty white flower is called Devil's Potato, or rubber vine, because of its twisting branches.

Fire is important in keeping the pine forest healthy. Without fire to thin out the trees, the older pines would crowd out the young seedlings. Fire also clears underbrush and makes room for young plants to grow. Some fires occur naturally, but rangers at the park also set fires. Fire fighters watch these *prescribed burns* closely to keep them under control.

Vegetation grows back quickly after a pine forest has burned. Often the forest is healthier because of the fire. Amanda examines the slash pine trees after a prescribed burn. The bark is made of many layers, so as the fire passed the trees, it burned only the outer layer of bark.

There is only one road that leads through the entire park—Main Park Road. It offers many surprises, such as a pair of black vultures sitting atop a nearby tree. Along the way, the vegetation differs from that of the interior. Here, dwarf cypress trees grow along the road.

Many creatures cross Main Park Road on the way from one part of the swamp to another. The gopher tortoise usually lives in pineland areas, while the poisonous water moccasin lives around fresh water. The water moccasin is also called a cottonmouth for its all-white throat.

Many of the most interesting sights along Main Park Road are very small. It takes good eyes to spot this tiny insect on a moon flower. A bright viceroy butterfly's bold colors make it easier to see. And a dainty spider web strung between blades of saw grass forms a pretty trap for unsuspecting insects!

No matter where you look in the Everglades, you'll find different types of flowers growing. Tiny white flowers called salt marsh mallow are named for the nearby marshes. The buttonbush is a favorite because it looks like a holiday ornament. And yellow plants called wild alamanda grow on vines along Main Park Road.

In another part of the park, a wooden boardwalk weaves through *Pa-Hay-Okee*, a saw grass marsh where various habitats meet. Pa-Hay-Okee is actually the Indian name for the Everglades—it means "grassy waters." From a dead branch nearby, a red-shouldered hawk watches as we stop to look at a display about the importance of the surrounding waters.

As water sinks into the ground, it settles in *aquifers*, which act as underground sponges. The aquifers absorb more water than all of southern Florida uses for drinking during the entire year! Common sights at Pa-Hay-Okee are the seas of saw grass and the pretty flowers, like the purple morning glory. Apple snail eggs are also seen clinging to the stems of plants just above the water line.

Miccosukee Indians once roamed throughout the Everglades, but now they have only one reservation, located along the northern boundary of the park and flanked by colorful totem poles. The Miccosukees are descendants of the Seminoles, who came here from north and central Florida many years ago. Here in southern Florida, the warm swampy environment brought about many changes in the Indians' lives. They built their homes, called *chickees*, with no walls, so cool breezes could pass through.

The Miccosukees are proud of their heritage.
Although they use modern items in their everyday
lives, they have managed to keep their customs
and traditions alive. On part of the reservation,
visitors can learn about some of these customs by
watching demonstrations put on by the Indians.
This Miccosukee is using traditional Indian tools to
carve ax handles.

Miccosukee women wear long full skirts to protect themselves from mosquitos. The traditional patchwork garments they make take many hours to create because they have such intricate designs. Miccosukee women also make beautiful necklaces from seeds and wooden beads.

Years ago, Indians traveled through the Everglades in dugout canoes carved from cypress trees. The front was pointed to push through the thick saw grass. A long thin pole was used to navigate through the shallow water. In a modern canoe, Rangers Kim and Dave explore Nine Mile Pond. They see interesting plants, like pulpy coco plums, along the water's edge.

The big alligators that live in Nine Mile Pond sometimes sun themselves on the banks. Although alligators seem similar to crocodiles, they are different. Crocodiles, like the one on the right, have pointed snouts, while alligators have rounded snouts. Crocodiles live only in brackish or salty water, while alligators prefer fresh water.

Important trees called red mangroves are found in coastal areas like Nine Mile Pond. When the tide comes in, soil and debris are trapped in the mangrove's strange-looking roots. This gradually creates new land. Mangroves have long, thin seed pods that drop off and are carried by the tides to new sites, where they may take root and begin to grow new trees. When seed pods and mangrove leaves begin to decompose in the water, they become food for fish.

Ranger Dave shows how to get a closer look at some of the small fish that feed along the shores of Nine Mile Pond. His large *seine net* comes up empty, but Amanda has better luck using a *dip net*. Along with some grass and pond moss, she scoops up a tiny fish!

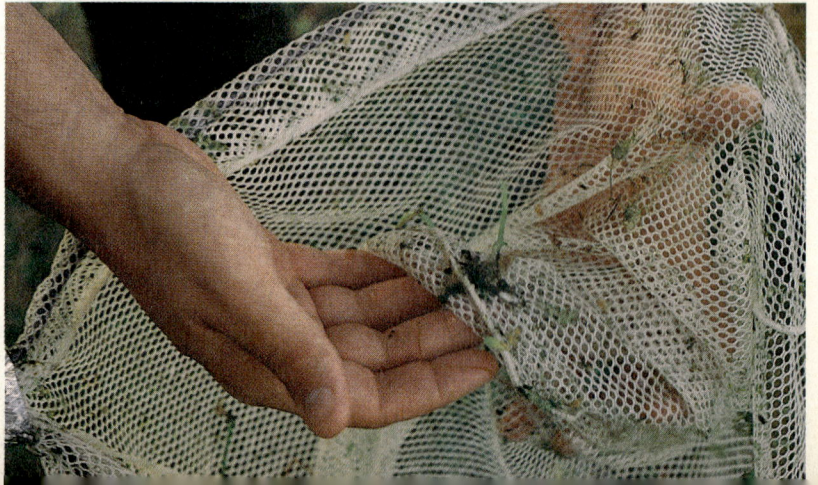

After spending hours walking through the Everglades, everyone is hungry. What better ending is there for a perfect day than having a picnic at the water's edge? Ranger Kim brings out the food and pours soda for everyone.

As we put our picnic gear away, the sun slips behind a tree island, and the sky turns golden. Alligators patiently wait for prey, fish swim silently, and the leaves and saw grass rustle in the evening breeze. Night falls, but the creatures in the Everglades continue to spin their web of life.